Poetic Imagery

Poetic Imagery

A Journey of Love

GLADYS DAE WEEKS

Copyright © 2018 by gladys dae weeks.

All rights reserved. No part of this book may be reproduced in any written, electronic, recording, or photocopying without written permission of the publisher or author. The exception would be in the case of brief quotations embodied on the pages where the publisher or author specifically grants permission.

Books may be purchased in quantity and/or special sales by contacting the publisher.

Mynd Matters Publishing
201 17th Street NW, Suite 300, Atlanta, GA 30363
www.myndmatterspublishing.com

ISBN-13: 978-1-948145-85-5 (pbk)

Cover illustration by JP Alexander

FIRST EDITION

To my two treasures, Ja and Pie.

BABIES
Wanting to grab you
And caress you
And kiss you
Until I'm dizzy

Contents

stress 9	mating season 35
native 10	epitome of indifference 36
assuage 11	motionless 37
infinite 12	rain on water 38
vows 13	comfort 39
figuring out 14	friendship 41
moments 16	serendipity 42
blue moon 17	my heart 43
visual seduction 18	social inadequacies 44
love comes softly 19	creation 45
let me 20	emotional detachment 46
delicious 21	sleep/still 47
dance for me 23	limited vision 48
unsure 25	mental image 49
love 27	the end is only the beginning 50
souls 28	
picnic 29	non-existent relationship 51
pixelated 30	
penetrating questions 31	32 degrees 53
silence 32	who could blame the moon? 55
seaside 33	
monkey wrench 34	seamless transition 58

stress

Write, letting the anger subside as the words drift across my mind into thought, serving to combat the war in my head, breathing quickly.

native

Amber flames dressed the night
As dancing feet pounded
Ancestors beat in time to
Moving feathers
Elements of true respect

assuage

Hiding in shadows he toils.
Crescent eyes sliding over seasons in his mind.
Longing. He dreams of black sand and purple sunsets.
He toils.
Circumventing sadness (he thinks).
Reflected in spools narrowly seeking mischief.
Forgetting starlit beaches, cloaked moons surrender to his eyes.
He toils. Hiding within work.
Joy receding with each tide sent through his body.
Sending waves through him.
Searching for a peace he'll never know.

infinite

Since our paths crossed
In the unmitigated space of time
You are unattached.
Each limb
hanging nefariously close to dissention
makes this moment visit forever.

VOWS

A voyage of discovery taken by two people

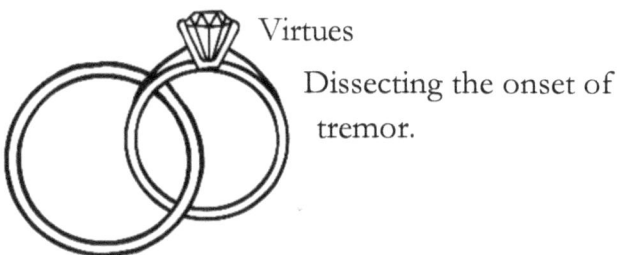

Virtues

Dissecting the onset of a tremor.

Figuring out

A tidal wave of love

Smoothed her neck.

Slowly.

Charges deemed settled.

Judging by actions

opposed to his words, a frame of reference,

genetically predisposed

this voyage of discovery

taken by both souls,

dissecting.

The porch under her feet moved.

The feeling, like a crush was delicious in its own

anticipatory way,

inviting strawberry sunsets

wrapping arms around her (vision),

fantasy.

Hearts lament safe.

Speechless, she trembled, refusing to say hello in

fear of saying good-bye.

Tapping into inspiration on the road less traveled

followed them, grabbing without thought

the passionate side

tailored to hear the meaning behind the words

figuring out

the significance of,

the core of.

A different version of the same story.

Consistency and fairness don't have to equal.

moments

When we separate

A bit

And my eyes happen upon you again

My breath catches

Overwhelmed by your incredible beauty

You smile –

And I am so eternally grateful

That I am the recipient

If only for a moment.

I smile too.

blue moon

tears triggered by guilt and sadness as her heart bleeds
slowly;
pain ripping through like electric currents.

visual seduction

Visual

Each held the other in their grasp

Locked.

Chest to chest, hip-to-hip, thigh to thigh,

unyielding, untraceable.

With his eyes, he consumed her, and she returned the favor,

his deep brown eyes warm.

All-seeing eyes that peered into the satin, silky walls

of her eternal soul.

Truly kissable lips.

Muscles filling a frame to perfection.

She acted out her fantasy.

Wild and scattered

Gentle touch

pleasing, proper

Seduction

love comes softly

Love comes softly

Creeping through your veins

Like the life of blood

Pulsating, invigorating your loins.

Beautiful.

Afraid of nothing but love itself

As soft as the wind on a cool summer's eve

tapping across your legs.

Love comes softly. Swiftly.

Vying for your heart,

Knowing it belongs elsewhere,

to someone else,

owned by the wind.

let me

let me.
allow me to seduce you;
let me warm your mind, your body, your spirit,
your soul.

let me seduce you.
bring a smile to your lips, a swagger to your hips.

let me seduce you
let me eat up each word as it rolls,
off yours into mine.
let me seduce you,
evoke, elicit, ignite.

and when the ambers are low,
and it's time to go,
leave me all aglow,
once more back in my box.
until it crumbles again.

delicious

You accuse me of not tasting you – yet.

Yet I have.

I taste you.

Every time

our eyes meet, moving from pensive to intense.

I breathe deeply, my soul satisfied.

Your eyes upon me, my body drinks you in.

You speak.

I internalize your visions as they inspire me to self reflect.

Your melodic voice enters my ears, creating goose bumps,

Flowing,

a soothing sensation that tickles my insides creating warmth all over.

I devour your mind as your honesty wraps around my heart causing my knees to quiver, my eyes to flutter like the butterflies in my stomach

traveling to a place that keeps me safe, secure, and gratified, due to your

smile.

Ever hungry in your presence, I'll continue to taste you until all of your

knowledge is

redefined in my smile.

dance for me

I dreamed that you danced for me.
Fantasized really,
about the way you moved.
I sat on my stool and watched you,
not wanting to stir,
mesmerized
by your motion,
admiring the deftness of each movement.
The song molded to your body; an instrument of power.
Dance for me,
my eyes kept saying.
Move while I watch.
Dance for me.
Roll and twist and grind and spin.
Dance for me.
Rock me baby.
And you did.
Closed your eyes and put me in your world.
And we danced together.
One step, two step, hand in hand. Aaaaahhhh.
How good you felt and smelled. Like fresh air
and early morning. Come closer.
Melt into me.
My hand on your back, we moved again. As one.
I nibble your ear as you lean into me.
Sweet.
Satisfaction so grand, there's no way to describe it.

I breathe again, not wanting the song to end; depth of emotion too strong.
I open my eyes to the sound of silence, wanting more.

unsure

i

stand before

you

naked, nude, raw.

ready.

i

stand before

you

invisible, vulnerable

afraid.

i

stand

at attention

hoping to catch your

attention.

i stand before you

ready to forego

all that i believe in

all that i hold

in my hand

yours

just

for

the

sake of.

lusting?

still,

i

stand

at

your

feet

waiting.

awaiting your approval, acceptance, hand

in delight

as you hold me

naked, nude, raw.

ready.

love

Beginning is easy.
Continuing is hard.
I wish it were like a record to play over when I
want to rewind
The song of life and keep singing.
Singing of Love.

souls

stand behind me and whisper
as I travel
far across
the earth
to a place
that
collapses time and space
under the influence
of the stars
in my eyes
while I sing
the song in my heart
created by
the movement of
mountains
pointing upwards.

picnic

As I sit here reminiscing,
arms wrapped around my knees
pulled up to my chest
filled with the warmth of your memories while the deer
dance across the sand,
I'm reminded of soda-filled crystal,
chicken-wrapped salads topped with chips and papaya juice
dripping on the monopoly of times gone past
while the waves lap against the moon
whose sun drifted off into the rainbow of your smile.

pixelated

The sky cried its fullness bursting through the clouds on picnic tables and blankets allowing only sprinkles of stars to keep the moon company

serenading the remnants on the beach watching the water sparkle.

Cascade. Ripple.

penetrating questions

Dripping with desire, wet with anticipation, I
await you.
You enter and I smile, our eyes meet-speaking
what we're both afraid to say.
Penetrating.
Questions.
Never leave your lips,
just hang in the air,
Stirring emotions too raw to face.
The stroke
of your eyes
over me, is really enough. Yet you
misunderstand all of this.
Lashes down, heart laden with the pain of
regrets, you turn slowly to leave,
not before a soft kiss brushes my lips.
Tears fall quietly that you never see driving
quickly to erase the memories that will surely
never be forgotten shared between two chairs, a
name plate, and brush.

silence

My heart breaks every time your name falls from
my mouth on deaf ears
behind me where hot breath used to be
replaced by tears where kisses once were
Now silence cuts the air.

seaside

The moon shone
as it massaged the shore.
Midnight fell.
Starless skies lay before
their eyes.
A lone bottle
drifted
riding the waves
as softly as his hands
caressing her feet.
Sweet sensations flowed.
Without warning
the clouds roared.

monkey wrench

My life was…pristine
Quiet, cool, serene, safe, riveted,
even steady
COMPLACENT,
Which turned to
doubt, chaos, dread, tumultuous, confusion,
chaotic,
heady
resulting in
soul-searching meditation, enlightenment,
disruption, pleasure, honey sweetness,
exploitation,
due to the fact that you are
Eclectic.
What's left is
Anticipation, exhilaration, serenity.

mating season

Like flirting fireflies

Your love illuminates

My dark forest with golden light

Blinking feelings

Exposed

Connecting dots of love

Our images become a sensation, traveling as

I feel the splendor and mystery of nature

Ecstatic to share my evening

Intent on capturing

All that glitters

epitome of indifference

Waterslide of tears
Ease the burden of self-loathing
Working it into exhaustion.
Trepidation.
Compassion not truly understood
A string of words
Throwing love around as if it means something
Alive and dead concurrently
Perhaps resounding more on the inside
Opposing harmonious forces
A danger only loneliness could evoke.
AM I ALONE IN THIS?
SOMETIMES LONLINESS MAKES SENSE

motionless

I spend all my time dreaming about what was or what should have been, and yet I arrive at the same spot. My life is stationary.

How can you anticipate the walk to come?

rain on water

Needing release from the thunder and lightning
Bellowed.
Tiny teardrops mixing with skin
Startled, he covered her in his arms
And it felt like
Rain on water

comfort

Where my arms can't reach, my voice floats across star-filled skies,

Sliding into your ears, my words overtake you. Can you hear them as they amuse your lobe, caress you, comfort you?

Dance upon your face.

Where my arms can't reach, my heart cradles you, holds your hands, rubs your head as sleep finds you,

Deep-still eyes refuse to flutter while you succumb to dreams.

Can you hear it beat with yours, comforting you as you comfort others?

Where my arms can't reach, my soul touches yours.

Where my arms can't reach, I stand with you,

My spirit aligns with your body, encapsulates you, keeping you warm and strong, ready to catch your tears, fears, sadness.

Where my arms can't reach, my feet carry me through deftly knit days

Until, they can hold you again.

friendship

Joys.
Progression.
Setbacks.
Near misses.
Sadness.
Comfort.

Acceptance.
Nonjudgmental.
Pleasure.
Strength.
Wisdom.

Valor.
Trust.
Love.
Friends. Life's gift of love.

serendipity

How enchanting were the stars

That shone in your eyes

The light

The night

A night of love

An enchanting moment on the water

When you had

The courage to love.

my heart

Widow peak windows watched

As trice gone

Monsoons reigned

spied through blurred visions

beguiled her stone heart, contradicting lucid tears.

Juxtapose

Wrapped in rainbows, hearts insanity tailspins

misery

as sleep pushes past.

Her naked body still

sunsets bleed her smile.

Pausing only long enough to negotiate new lucid

tears

hydrating

Heart pangs heart pangs

My heart

hoping beyond all.

Be still my heart be still.

Is this how we should love?

social inadequacies

Opulent in a romantic sort of way

Tongue-tied you walk away

Remove

Remorse

Extendibility following

She knew then what she was up against

creation

Silence ceases as rain began to fall
Harmonic dodecaphonic techniques did not cool
things off
Causing goose bumps to take over.
As the storm continued,
truth slipping haphazardly through her fingers,
she curled under him, finding beauty in the world.

emotional detachment

He walks away, lust satisfied in the spasms of reality
already forgotten as she smiles floating in his shadow,
spent,
anxious for soft hands again
though
afraid her emotions scare (him).

He drives aimlessly reaching the tip of the world
Ignoring the call of the Longtail as she cries his name, (haunting him).
Lost between the raindrops pounding the slate roof
she turns just in time to
catch a glimpse
Of his soul as he returns it (to stone).
Not understanding that her emotional attachment
is her emotional detachment
each time he leaves (her)
unanswered call in his wake.
Walks away.
He walks away.

sleep/still

Lingering air of disappointment surrounds me
as the pain of your words
cover my body like a tattered blanket, though
softly spoken
hurt.
in direct contrast to your touch, for the first time
felt like love-making
as your soft kisses traveled my spine.
You stopped to remind me of your taste.
I roll over to catch up-unable to find your smile, I
surrender to your desire.
Yet you leave too soon for me to pretend it's
okay. In its stead,
I ramble
To cover
The pain of your words
Finding comfort from your t-shirt
I've donned in your absence.
When I breathe in. Still.
The scent of you
still lingers.
Caressing my dreams in slumber.

limited vision

One cold blistery day
The ancestors whispered
Hairs standing tall-tingled
She hid behind it
Ignoring the tugging of her heart
Steady
Beating as love slipped in
Equity moved to the place
Limited field of vision

mental image

If I kissed you on your bottom lip,
If I looked into your eyes
If I trailed our journey on your backbone
Will it release a different kind of truth?

the end is only the beginning

He took her love tenderly into his hand
Turned it over in his mind too.
Squeezed it a bit.
Not hard, not tightly, just so, just enough.
Placed a kiss in the center
of her palm.
Held it so
trying to hold on
To time lost.
Lost time.
Forgotten while the wind caressed the leaves that
blew in its wake
landing on the doorstep of love.

non-existent relationship

Caught between two worlds

he waivered, teetering on the verge of distinction.

Just moments before the fall, calmly, love surfaced, coming slowly without limits.

It bloomed, slightly, hid, surfaced again.

The sudden allegiance overwhelmed him, yet, he yearned for more.

His heart swelled, causing remembrance of pain like the ocean, endless,

left behind.

Again, his soul failed him, though this time he was prepared.

Suddenly, her mind took flight, and he followed, catching her like the wind in a storm of lost souls.

He grabbed her for comfort, not just hers. Love wrecked.

His heart too, bled, but for disparate reasons.

His thrown against a dilemma, too difficult to grasp without divulgence; too personal to shed under the guise of stars lost in his eyes: a broken carriage; one lost wheel, one overturned, one left behind; the last of course, holding on, pretending to be important.

And so, they began to dream,

Independently together, of a life uninterrupted,

now stolen while others slept peacefully in the dark colony, wakening alone, not too soon to judge,

Love, a storm in his heart.

32 degrees

As

He stood facing her, eye level of the sea, torrid thoughts circling,

she blinked twice, eyes full of depth watching vigilantly for the fall.

Words tumbled forth. Between, around and over them.

Her feelings screaming inside, afraid of rejection; intimidated only by his perseverance of love undetermined by his actions.

In reality, that was their life. Up at dawn, reversed at sunset, alive only with the moon casting shadows on their lust. It was their symbol for excuses, decimated in whispers as they huddled in their need for each other.

Unspoken desire touching their skin, pouring off like water washing over sand moist and receding; surfacing again like laps in secret.

Stolen moments used wisely.

As if it were their last.

Their relationship thrived as such; tea, a book, small talk.

Easily it moved, passing through streams (flowing into calm waters) and small obstacles, life intertwined with life, tossing out devices to equip themselves for survival. Like children schooled together, they learned to adapt.

They swayed and cooed; their laughter crystal and sweet; pastries awaiting the delight of decadent chocolate lovers.

Subsequently, the smiles grew wide like the mouth of a river, feeding into greater temptation.

Gradually but cleverly the waters ran deeper, an abyss of power raging—becoming ingrained, slanting through their veins growing rapidly as flowers in spring saturated in the love of water and sun and moons, full.

Substantial substantiation was the glint seen in her eyes, gait light and carefree; his sheltered under the vest of disbelief.

Expectations.

This is where he left it.

who could blame the moon?

it would be easy to blame the moon for her unrest, nestled in the sky, stars speckled, looking innocent;

discarding

responsibility for the paradox that existed over the priceless gift of love; her insides churning when his voice breaks the silence.

It would be easy to blame the moon for her unrest, settling in the waves, wrestling the sand awake; anxiously walking on tiptoes to afraid to disturb the silence.

Her heart fluttered, lifted, naturally, not knowing it was love that caused the ripples of the sea; washing over freshly painted toes ready for flight. Her heart beat faster, the song of the birds startling, their screeches a warning of danger.

Were they too, afraid of love?

Who could blame the moon?

A solitary tear dropped, confirming her displeasure, yet relief. Dictation faltered.

Hollow syllables fell to the ground. What after all was left to be said?

More tears spilled, a graphic representation of the distance between their hearts now understood through mishap and the placement of her heart; the only thing left to salvage.

This time.

it would be easy to blame the moon for her unrest, a massive plot, sporadically appearing, ripping the sky; immense sphere tripping over the sun in its haste to showcase its splendor, kissing the stars, seducing the behavior as if it's able to love, mending her heart along the way.

Kinetic, changing, parting, constant flux, avoiding-information stored in the suitcase,

(you know the one), baggage; weaving in and out of heartache like traffic.

Foremost, everything is what you get used to; therefore, she led a life of sterility, trying to clean up the past, present and future in unison.

The flagrant side prevailing, in its dismay, forcing her to face life with a new commitment for survival, won the fight.

Life is calling me.

Who could blame the moon?

seamless transition

IS A MENTAL THING

WHAT I WANT YOU TO KNOW

ENCAPSULATES EVERY MOMENT OF MY JOURNEY

WHEN YOU STEP BACK AND LOOK AT YOUR WORK IT OFTEN SPEAKS TO

THE WAY YOU UNDERSTAND LIFE.

www.ingramcontent.com/pod-product-compliance
Lightning Source LLC
Chambersburg PA
CBHW030104100526
44591CB00008B/263